THREE WORDS

Live Your Legacy

Becky Scott Sharpe

ISBN-13: 9798987812624 (Kindle edition)
ISBN-13: 9798987812648 (Digital online E-Book)
ISBN-13: 9798987812655 (Paperback)

Printed in the United States of America

To all my co-pilots, but especially my parents, Donna and Charles, who taught me confidence and that it was ok to just be me. To Michael, Tyson, Lucas and Lilly who inspire me to be better every day. To my brothers, Stuart and CR whose unwavering support lifts me up and motivates me to do and be better. I love you all.

CONTENTS

FOREWORD

The first draft of this book was over 100k words, 27 chapters and approaching 200 pages. Then a business friend, Nancy Fox, and I discussed the negative impact of being overly verbose, droning on, talking to hear yourself, well, talk. Both of us greatly appreciate succinctness. During our discussion, I realized I started my book-writing project with an unconscious bias, had read or heard somewhere that a legitimate book needed to be long. Having recently read The Lion Hunters Guide to Life (Varty) I knew that a short read could also be a deep, impactful, and complex one, so started the process of deleting words, then paragraphs and even chapters. I wanted the reader to be able to get through this book on a short (under 2-hour) flight.

This book is for professionals who are open to discovering how to live a life with joy, meaning and balance in it, as who you are at your best. It is for leaders who are curious how to learn from and appreciate people who bring different skills and experiences. If you have worked hard, been promoted, and taken on more and more responsibilities only to find that more does not feel much better than less, join the crowd!

If you have moments during which you feel there is a void and want to discover how to fill that space with a positive mindset and with people and experiences that bring you peace and joy, read on. If you want to discover your best self and the three words that describe you at your best, pick your journaling method (pen and paper, or electronic) and start writing!

As you contemplate and refine your three words and discover their related stories, every experience will appear to have a lesson to offer, customized to you. The more you think and write about each of them, the quicker your growth and evolution will be. As you identify the things that keep you from being your best and decide to spend less time with bad habits, your stress will diminish. You will learn the power of asking for and receiving help and the joy when you give it unconditionally.

Finally, you will have the chance to reframe negative experiences so that you can focus on what they taught you, not be held hostage by them. As you shift your mindset more positively, you will begin to make decisions that support your legacy word or words with ease.

INTRODUCTION

I love the restaurant Vui's Kitchen. The food is fresh and yummy and Vui, the owner, exudes joy and appreciation. Anytime I'm lucky enough to run into her I have the lingering feeling that everything is gonna be just fine and that there's some excellent news coming my way. Positivity seems to emanate from her like a force field. If you're ever in Nashville, go there. Yes, hot chicken is a unique experience but if I had to choose my last meal, Vui's Pho and homemade, steamed dumplings with chili oil would be at the top of the list. After going there for food for years, I realized I also went for the dose of positivity I got from watching Vui interact with people. Her smiling eye contact or upbeat words are so natural. Some people just have that magic.

It was sitting at Vui's, with my friend Brian Gleason, that I was first introduced to the three words. I had recently soloed in a helicopter and Brian had decided to learn to fly airplanes and we were sharing our awe of being 'up there'. Brian and I are both CEOs and are wired similarly – focused on the macro, the long term, while making sure the details, the day-to-day, are delegated to those with a different skill set than we have. It's important to both of us that everyone in our businesses treats others with respect and through a filter that is based in love. I think that macro approach is what drew us both to learn to fly. We both saw and related the flying metaphor to running a functional business with a great culture: when it comes to flying, every job, whether completed by ground control or a small bolt tucked away deep in an engine, is vital. Both of us spent a significant amount of time on creating business cultures in which everyone felt important.

We'd been in a business group called Vistage for many years, learning from speakers and each other and sharing what kept us up at night. I had been contemplating getting a business coach and knew Brian had had one. When I asked if he would hire a coach again, he paused for few seconds and thought deeply, then said he would, but only because of one thing he'd learned. His coach had asked him to think about what three words described him at his best. Then, over the next several months, she and he would discuss the words and why they were his.

We spent the next 30 minutes sharing our words, I kept changing mine, but saw a pattern emerging. More on my words later...

At a stoplight, after lunch, I started thinking about my words and if I could incorporate that concept into a class at Vanderbilt's Owen Graduate School of Management where I guest lectured a few times each semester. If thinking about your three words was the most valuable thing a successful CEO had gleaned from an expensive executive coach, surely the MBA students would benefit too.

I decided that before my next lecture at Owen, I would review my outline and add the 'three words' question to my introductory section during which I asked the students to think about their mindsets. In that section I ask them to think about memories that serve them and ones that don't. Now I was going to ask them to associate their three words with stories that bubbled to the surface when I prompted 'what is one of your earliest happy memories?'

For me, taking time to consider opposites helps me see blind spots, unconscious biases, and assumptions. If I had taken time to think about my three words in graduate school, I might have experienced less stress and anxiety about my struggle with accounting and statistics; 'analytical' is NOT one of my three words. Had I gone deep with my three words I would have had more acceptance of - and appreciation for - how I am naturally wired.

For each word that describes us at our best, there is an opposite, a shadow word, that when revealed loses its power to influence us so negatively as when it's hidden, ignored, or not talked about. There is also an ideal state, a legacy word or words, that can guide us toward a more fully-evolved and peaceful state of mind.

Thanks to my friend sharing the concept of three words and my mother's Jungian influence, I saw this book's content flash before me in a few stop lights. Incorporating the three words and their opposites as well as legacy words with the powerful impact of journaling would become my way of helping people create a filter through which they could contemplate decisions so that they could experience more joy and gratitude than shame and regret.

This book is for you, leader, if, you want to find out who you really are at your best and how to pause before making decisions so that you benefit from your choices instead of having to continuously apologize and clean up messes that could have been avoided. You will get to know the experiences, the stories, that have impacted you and learn how to shift your mindset to one more often in appreciation and gratitude rather than focusing on what is negative.

Have a journal nearby so that you can start writing!

PART ONE

Three Words

Three Words

What three words describe you at your very best? Are you kind, generous and focused? Are you rested, light-hearted and loving? I love asking people what their three words are. Their answers usually come quickly, and I see them having an 'ah-ha' moment as one person says 'driven' and someone next to them says 'grateful'. There are no right or wrong answers. Some people like to rhyme or sort of rhyme: Kind, Grind, Devine. Others like alliteration: Generous, Grateful and Goofy. My three words are FIT, FUN and FOCUSED. Every day I ponder how I am living them. The more I think about them, the more my mind helps me make decisions that strengthen them and signals me to hang out with people who feed and encourage the three words that describe me at my best. I spend time doing things 'in' them when I think and journal about them regularly.

The more I think about my three words, the more I start and end my day with a positive thought about them. What was your first thought this morning? Was it generally positive, like 'I'm going to go for a walk and start my day moving?' Or, was it a negative thought, an internal scoff or a shameful recollection? Being aware of what thoughts come to you right as you wake up and just before you drift off, will help you understand if your brain is feeding your positive or negative ones.

If you are getting more negative thoughts than positive, then taking time to read, journal or think of a positive experience, when you wake up and right before you go to sleep, will help rewire your brain in a direction that will bring you more serenity. Then, the actions and thoughts that are good for you will come with more frequency.

To enhance my word **fit**, I started practicing moving when talking on my cell to move more; now, when I get a phone call, I hear my inner voice suggesting that I stand up and walk instead of staying seated. I've logged thousands of miles by walking and talking or listening to a podcast or audible book and am sure my 105-year-old self will be appreciative of the muscle tone and flexibility that was the result of years of a fit focus. Thinking about what makes up being fit led me to add yoga and sauna-ing to my routine. I wear a Fitbit and an Apple Watch, and am motivated, not pressured, to hit my daily goals because 'fit' is truly one of my three words. Thinking about what defines 'fit' for me helps me identify and act on things that support my goal to be as fit as possible. Since I identified the word, I find myself doing things, like parking far away from my desired location, and getting a longer walk. Or doing laps at an airport while waiting to board a plane. I'm not as tempted to eat junk food, but instead, feel good, not denied, when I choose an apple as a snack. When I am fit, strong, flexible, well-nourished, hydrated and rested, I show up better for my family, friends and co-workers. I know that if I'm out of shape, weak, or unrested, I don't show up as my best.

You'll know you've found your words when, without much effort, you begin to find intersections between them. To add **fun** to the everyday, I like to put on some upbeat music when I'm doing chores and immediately feel like I'm 'getting' to vacuum, instead of 'having' to vacuum and have an upbeat attitude as I get some steps in while boogying down to some 80s dance music. Listening to music adds a fun component to an otherwise mundane task for me. I like to go for a long walk or hike and ponder or focus on a topic. Moving and thinking often results in an 'ah ha' that doesn't come as quickly (or at all) if I sit at a desk under florescent lights and try to problem solve. It's just how I'm wired. I have friends who are the exact opposite. They are more creative when not moving. The idea is to identify the words that describe what makes you feel great and think most clearly. You might need a clean, tidy surrounding that's quiet, or a noisy, active coffee shop where you feel alive. There is no right or wrong way to feel energized, the key is knowing what works for you.

I like to laugh and find humor in all sorts of things. When I'm having fun, loving life, seeing things as goofy or quirky, just enjoying being alive, I'm at my best. I heard a speaker talk about the incredibly healing and cathartic impact keeping a humor journal had been for her and started one immediately. I add to it every month, noting something that I found funny. When I go back and read it, I get a nice chuckle and recall something I would have forgotten otherwise. Some of those entries include:

My Mom meaning to say 'iPad mini', but instead saying 'minipad' when talking to the salesperson at the Verizon store: "I have a minipad…right here in my purse."

Lilly (my daughter, at 5) referring to the sushi at our favorite place: "it's almost always never fishy."

Crazy squirrel leaping onto my bird feeders – mad as a hatter!

After I started keeping a humor journal, I began noticing funny, lighthearted things more often. If fun is one of your words then journaling about things you found fun or funny will energize you.

I know that when I can find the lightness in a situation, I am more likely to find creative solutions. I'm also very quick to make things light, even hard conversations. Like my approach to reacting to bad drivers, which is to imagine they are having a VERY bad day, instead of intentionally trying to make me mad, I would prefer to be easy and light, imagining they just got some awful news instead of letting their ridiculous driving ruin my moment. Even with touchy situations, I'd rather just notice than be mean and dogmatic. I have found that humor helps me calm down, be less fearful and more curious. Think about situations you've been in and how you dealt with discomfort or mean people in such a way that you felt proud. What's a word that describes you in that moment?

When I think, slow down, and **focus** from ten thousand feet before I act, the results are simply better. My tendency to knee jerk, to act fast, has had unintended negative consequences. But, when I take even a few seconds to pause, think, breath and focus, I perform and interact better. To focus, I need a clean, quiet place with no distractions. So, I take time to tidy up around me before diving into something that needs my focus. I like to have my noise cancelling air pods in with some baroque or Icelandic classical music playing softly. Feeding your three words, really living them, requires acknowledging what you need and letting people who can impact your surroundings know. Whether it's quiet, noise, being alone or in a group, getting more familiar with what brings you a sense of calm and confidence will help you identify and then focus on the three words you choose to describe you in your best state of mind and body.

◆ ◆ ◆

Take time to contemplate and then live your three words and notice the impact when you are spending time living them. Change your environment so that it has more of what you need. Share your three words with people close to you and ask them what theirs are

PART TWO

Your Shadow Words

Your Shadow Words

There is, as Carl Jung would say, a shadow side to your best self. And I've found that the same applies to your three words. Think about what their opposites are. Mine are weak, wounded, and worried. If you like alliteration or rhyme, pick opposite words that start with the same letter or rhyme with three words that describe you at your best. Sometimes I use sick, sad, and scattered instead for my shadow words.

The idea is to understand the words that are the opposites to those that describe you at your best, so that you can recognize situations to avoid, stop a bad habit before it fully develops and identify people who are more likely to encourage and invite time and energy in shadow-enhancing, negative or dangerous experiences or thoughts.

I just don't feel good physically or mentally if I'm overweight or out of shape; that's why **weak** is one of my shadow words. It's important to understand that shadow words are not meant to criticize others. That's a subtlety that's important to understand. Your shadow words are just that, yours. For others, the same words might energize them. For example, if one of your shadow words is extraverted or introverted, that does not mean people who are either are not good or right. Knowing what other peoples' words are will help you communicate more effectively with them.

If someone tells me I upset them because I came across as uncaring or light-hearted about something that was heavy for them, it will weigh on me for days, causing me to wake up in the middle of the night and lose focus as I replay whatever happened. When I feel **wounded**, become defensive and embrace a victim mentality, the results are not good for me; I lose my sense of lightness and humor. My energy level plummets when I am sad. When I allow myself to do too many things at the same time, checking email while on a call or listening to a podcast or audio book more than to the birds, I lose focus and begin to feel **worried**, like there is a bad energy flowing through me.

What are your signals that you are embracing your shadow words instead of those that bring you joy and a sense of ease?

◆ ◆ ◆

Use a pencil to list your three words and your three shadow words in your journal so that as you explore your words you can edit them easily!

Thought prompt: Why did you choose each word? Think of an experience that came to you and write it in your journal.

Journaling prompts:

Today when I woke up, my first thought was….

How did your first thought impact your mindset, more positively or negatively?

Tonight, before I fall asleep, I want to think about…

Why did you pick that idea as your last thought of the day?

Where do you spend more thought and experience, in joy and curiosity or anxiety?

What activities can you do more or less of so that your three positive words feel more powerful than your shadow ones?

Getting To Know Each Word

You'll know you've identified your words when you begin to associate your actions and thoughts with them. After one of my workshops, a participant said, *'how did you get me to dream about my words?!"*

Not only will you dream about them, but you will also start to think about them when reading a book, listening to a podcast or lecture or in simple quotes. If you take time to go through pictures from your early childhood and ask older people in your family to tell you what they remember about that time, you will be exposed to stories, some of which will align with your words.

The more you think about your words, the more you will, without effort, find examples of them all around you. You will learn to pause BEFORE you act and decide if what you are about to say or do aligns with your positive or shadow words. You will develop the skill to choose actions and reactions that align with the words that describe you at your best and your shadow words will, well metaphorically, stay in the shadows.

Great businesspeople know that if you want to manage something, you must measure it. As you track your mindset, noting if you are trending more positive or negative, you will know which words are getting the attention.

◆ ◆ ◆

When you feel a connection between your three words and whatever you are experiencing, honor the connection by validating it mentally. You can silently think 'I am seeing a connection'.

Happy Memories

What is your earliest **happy** memory? The memory can be something you remember or could be a story you heard or one you saw in a picture of you as a child. Reflect until you find one of you, as young as you can recall, when there was something happening that was good. Write all you can about it; who are you with? What are you doing? Add as many details as you can.

One of my earliest memories was captured in a picture. It's fine if you don't remember the memory but experience via photo, video, or story after-the-fact. In this little black and white photo, I'm about 10 months old and my dad is holding me. He looks so young and very happy. As I studied the picture, I noticed that I'm holding on to his earlobe. I imagine how comfortable and safe I felt being held by this person so much larger than I who was fine with my tiny hand clinging to his earlobe. I journaled about the photo and anytime I read that journal entry or see that photo, I feel a sense of deep love. Then I had an idea. I took a picture of the picture and sent it to my dad, who was in his late 80's at the time.

"Dad, do you remember this?" I queried.

"Yes, of course, Beck! We were visiting your grandparents in Memphis and there was a lot of noise in the house. You were getting a bit anxious. Your bottom lip started to stick out, so I picked you up and we went outside. You exhaled audibly, calming, and reached up and grabbed my earlobe. Your mother came out and took that photo."

Call your relatives and ask them questions about memories or photos and journal what they say. You will gain insight and information and they will feel connected and heard.

All happy memories you journal about are available to you anytime you want to re-live them by reading what you've written. Add titles to your memories: *On the farm*; *At the Beach*; *Soccer Practice*; *Cooking with Granddad*. You get it.

Create a room of happiness by journaling about what happiness looks like to you. If you could walk into a room of you at your happiest, what would you see in there? How would your joyful memories be displayed? I've heard people describe their positive memories like artwork, a sculpture of a hug with a grandmother, a movie picture from a summer camp at a lake, framed photos of memories you have but that weren't captured on film.

You can do this exercise for different times in your life. When you have a new, happy experience, take a moment to journal about it and think how you'd like it displayed in a room of happiness. Schedule time to take a mental break and read your journal. Add details as they come and let yourself get lost in there.

After journaling for years, I began to lose my motivation to write, and had a bit of writer's block. I was able to relaunch my journaling by purchasing a new journal and titling it 'Dear Great, Great, Great....' The idea was to write letters, stories, share thoughts with a great, great, great relative, someone I'm not going to know. Thinking that this person in the future might find and then read my journal of what brings me joy, what mistakes I've made and how I learned from them, rejuvenated my desire to write more often. So, if you find yourself with writers' block, imagine someone 100 years from now and tell them what you want them to know.

◆ ◆ ◆

Take clarity breaks and journal about things that bring you joy. Start writing to a 'great, great, great' future relative.

The Mindset of Fear

"Daddy, there's a monster in my closet."

"Are you sure?"

"Yes, every time you turn the light out it starts making a noise."

"Ok, let's see what happens when I turn the light out."

Click – light out.

Noise ensues.

"See?" I point out.

"Yes, let me show you what it is." My dad proceeded to show me how central air conditioning worked and that the noise wasn't related to the lights being out, but with the quiet associated with going to bed.

"I'm still scared."

"That's ok. If I leave the closet light on will that help?"

"Yes." I said, a bit less than enthusiastic. But it did.

"You can always leave the light on, honey. That's your call. What's important is knowing that you are safe."

"Will you turn it off after I fall asleep?"

"Do you want me to?"

"No." Of this I was very sure.

"Then I won't."

That was a big ask for my energy-conserving, budget conscious, 'don't turn up the heat, put a coat on' father. But he had some intuition that prioritized not making his 5-year-old go to sleep scared, so instead helped her to find reality instead of getting stuck in an imagination that was not serving her.

What my dad did was listen and accept, instead of arguing with me about, my fear; he showed me what I was hearing and then gave my fear a place to exist while reducing its power over me. He let me keep the light on without shame. To this day I can fall asleep easily and sleep deeply pretty much anywhere. Sometimes I leave the light on.

One of my memories that I've journaled about is of that experience. It is a black and white pencil drawing of a little girl in pajamas standing in front of an HVAC return, a quizzical look on her face, raggedy Ann hanging from her hand. My Dad is partially in the picture, his legs and shadow, his hand holding hers. When I re-read my journaled description of that scene from my youth, it reminds me that anytime I experience fear, I will benefit from doing some data searching before I allow fear to engulf me. Often, when I take time to data gather, my assumptions, especially if they are of a bad outcome, get proven wrong. It's often just the metaphorical nighttime sounds of HVAC.

Journaling prompts:

What stories do you remember from your childhood?

What did you learn from them?

What would you tell your great, great, great future relative?

What would you want them to learn from you?

Core Values and Mindset

What are your personal core values? They will align with your three words. Are you clear on what your core values are and are you living them?

A business friend of mine told me one of his core values was **integrity** and then I watched him lie and cheat a team member. When I called him out on it, he made excuses, justifying his dishonesty. I was not surprised when, over time, his business and personal life went more and more south. He seemed to be aging more quickly than most, dark circles appearing under his eyes as he kept a lie alive and embraced actions that were in direct opposition to one of his alleged core values. Oh, what a tangled web...

It's not always that way, sometimes the hypocrites get away with it. But I think that they never experience the level of joy and happiness they would if they were being true to their core values. They spend time and energy hiding the truth; they are acting in a way that they'd prefer stay secret not because they are private people, because they don't want to get caught doing something they know to be wrong. Some have lists of things they don't want to get caught doing. What a complicated way to live. When your gut or instinct is that you don't want people to see or know something, not a private thing, like you in the shower, but something you don't want to get 'caught' doing, you are getting a valuable insight, that you are making choices that feed your shadow words.

Listening to your gut is a simple way to analyze if you are contemplating doing something that will not bring you happiness in the long run. Ignoring it, your instinct, puts you at risk for experiencing the backlash that will happen when you find yourself defending your actions as you say or think 'I knew you would get mad if you found out. That's why I didn't tell you'.

We have a free tool, that inner voice, that can lead us straight to joy and happiness and, I believe, is a super food towards evolving into the best version of us. Sadly, many people ignore it, paying attention instead to the gloom-inducing, negative, judgy voice. If you take the time to listen to both or, even better, journal and contemplate what you're hearing before you act, you'll likely see a pattern.

When I hear from my negative voice, I acknowledge what I'm hearing, but, more often than not, I choose not to act on it. 'Come on Becky, it's just a few glasses of wine. You're still ok to drive'. For me, acknowledging the bad, dangerous, or negative thoughts of doing or saying things that are dangerous, not good for me or my relationships, makes them less powerful. Instead of trying not to hear them, by hearing them, but not acting on them, I find that those thoughts come less frequently and with less volume. It's as though the negative voice has given up on trying to convince me to act.

I think lies create mental scar tissue, tightness, a tugging discomfort that we might get caught. And the more we tell them, the thicker the tissue and more likely we will experience a mental lack of flexibility, or range of motion. We know that to heal, say, a hamstring strain, requires some rest, some ice and maybe even some massage to get rid of the scar tissue so that it heals without limiting our range of motion.

When we get into the habit of lying, hiding or misleading and then justify our actions instead of slowing down, being responsible, applying some mental ice, by chilling out and being honest, we increase the odds that we will get into a routine of obfuscation, our mental scar tissue limiting our ability to think broadly and with a smooth and open mind.

What if what you said or did was broadcast for everyone to see? I don't mean you dancing in your underwear, I mean that you have an instinct that someone who matters would be upset or worse, if they knew or witnessed something you were about to do. Would you do it anyway and hope they didn't find out? If so, you have an opportunity to strengthen your discipline, improve your actions and mindset or to maintain a weaker version of yourself. You have a chance to eliminate the formation of the scar tissue that comes when you ignore your insight.

It may sound tough, but it's something I've seen over and over: people who prioritize selfishness and an inability to regulate themselves over an impact they know will be negative to others. There's a simple way to work on this. Pause before acting or saying something and think 'will the people who I care about be negatively impacted by what I'm about to say or do?'. Then make your choice and think about if it makes you happy, scared, joyful or frightened. Your mindset is your choice, and your choices impact your mindset.

From the book, *Conscious Leadership* (Dethmer, Chapman and Klemp), I learned a great way to contemplate or review my actions and thoughts: are they above or below the line? I'm simplifying this fabulous read, so please buy the book, but in a nutshell, the idea is to recognize where you are – above or below the line – and then to think about what role you are playing in the situation, accepting yourself for the role you are playing and where you are, and, finally, deciding if you are willing to shift. Can you step into a love-based decision instead of a me-based one?

Arg! Ownership of a situation. It's so much easier to finger point and blame others, but, alas, at least for me, the more I see that my thoughts and actions belong to one person, me, the more I am able to accept that my state of mind is my choice. And, I want to live a life of joy and happiness, not spite, anger and regret. Letting go of the outcomes is a great way to find balance in mindset. There is a resulting overall sense of ease when we focus on what we control and not on the outcomes.

My core values are: Loyalty, Optimism, Very Fun (why do 'fun' when you can do 'very fun'?) and Equity. I don't stick to them all the time, but boy, when I have moments when I am fully in them, I feel amazing, like I am doing what I'm meant to, showing everyone love and reveling in their successes.

I was wearing a top with the word 'LOVE' on it while doing hot yoga one day when I noticed the word backwards in the mirror – EVOL- and had an epiphany. 'To evolve positively and creatively requires love'. I want to evolve, to grow into the best possible version of me. To do so, I believe, requires me to try to live in a love-focused way. Would a love-based person continue a phone conversation and ignore the clerk at a store or put the phone conversation on hold and greet that person with a smile and a sincere question about how their day was going?

How about as a boss? Can you fire someone from a position of love? Can you quit a job or share hard feedback in a loving way?

Journaling prompts:

What are your core values and why?

For each, note if you are making decisions more in harmony (+) or conflict (-) with them.

What secrets are you keeping from whom and why?

◆ ◆ ◆

List, review and think about your core values and whether your actions (and thoughts!) support or are in conflict with them. Journal about any secrets you are hiding.

The Room of Doom and Gloom

We all have negative experiences. The pros, I've witnessed, own them, learn from them, but are not defined by them. Like letting go of things out of your control, accepting that bad things happen but not dwelling on them will bring you peace.

In December of 2010, I had shoulder surgery. Recovering at home, I was more tired and in pain than I'd expected. We were due to drive to Atlanta to see my husband's family for Christmas and my intuition was screaming at me not to go. I thought about it, almost said something, but my over-functioning self stepped in and threw me to the wolves.

I had no idea what OxyContin was, having very rarely taken anything stronger than over-the-counter Tylenol. Once in Atlanta I was offered, and gladly accepted a glass of wine after dinner. The pain lightened. I had another and then 2 more. The next thing I knew, I had totally lost my mind, was watching myself yell at my husband that his family was 'full of white trash'. It was a complete cluster fuck. I had no idea that mixing opioids with alcohol was a no-no and doing so had removed any filter I had, leaving my husband, understandably furious, his family stunned and mad and me embarrassed and excuseless. I had nothing.

I called and apologized, but don't think they ever really got over it. I know that my mistake was just that, a mistake. I didn't go there to insult anyone, but I had more than accomplished that. I felt sick at my stomach off and on for days and did not get any support from the people I insulted. They accepted my apology, but never checked in with me or expressed an understanding of the negative impact on me the experience had had. And I was too ashamed to say anything that implied I, too, had been wounded by the event and needed some grace. No one asked me about how I was feeling, and I felt like a little girl for wanting them to know I was suffering with guilt and shame and would benefit from hearing 'We get you and that wasn't you. Let it go. We have." I got silence, was not invited to visit, as I recall, again, and felt completely alone and not at all forgiven.

My shame gained strength and power, hanging over me like a dark cloud, whispering to me that I was no good and deserved no forgiveness, coming to me in waves and making me space out during meetings and lose focus. Then, one day, during a swim, I lost all desire to continue, got out of the pool after just a few minutes, walking like a wet, wounded dog to the locker room, where I felt a mope coming on. I was in full-on victim mode. Sitting, droopy headed in the sauna, wanting to cry, but, for some reason, unable to let go and release, I decided I needed to forgive myself, learn from my mistake and not depend on others to move on. I focused on what I could control, which did not include other people's thoughts or behaviors, took a deep breath, let it go and headed back to the pool.

I never mixed alcohol and a prescription drug again, and, when I had my hip replaced, I took the narcotics for as little time as possible, adding bleach to the half full bottle and shaking it, to eliminate the chance that such a dangerous thing would even be in my house. It would be 15+ years later when the shameful Sackler family would be exposed, and during that time all three of our children lost friends to unintentional overdose of the shit. If you don't know who the Sackler family is, check https://www.forbes.com/profile/sackler/?sh=2a6775975d6.

When we rely on others to release us, we are likely to get stuck waiting. I am not encouraging you to avoid deep relationships, but I am suggesting that you think about if and where you are stuck and waiting for someone else to set you free. **Set yourself free**. When others do so, too, it's gravy. But don't depend on another person's decision to forgive you or not to allow yourself to move on.

If you have been impacted negatively by people, consider forgiving them. The amazing people who have been willing to share how they forgave people for their negative experiences, grievances, and injuries with me have taught me there is another way; there is a way to set and be set free.

Some people have had face-to-face conversations; others have written letters or emails; some have had a ceremony, burning a piece of paper that had the whole affair detailed on it. One woman forgave someone who had long since died and said she felt like a weight had been lifted. None of this, forgiving, is a new concept, but I think it's one we can easily forget to think about as we dash through life. Authors like Brene Brown have opened a new concept to the world, the power in being vulnerable. Somewhere along the way, I learned that business leaders had to be tough and didn't need things like forgiveness, that being open or showing emotions was a sign of weakness. That's just malarky.

In my journal, I created a mental space to put my mistakes, gaffs, blunders, and missteps, especially if they are weighing on me, waking me up in the middle of the night or distracting me. I call it the **room of doom and gloom**. It looks like a very scary, old world, prison cell, cold and dark, rats scrambling in the corners, the drip of cold water in the distance. The door leading into this nasty place, is thick and made of ancient-looking stone, a small opening at eye level has 4 rusty, iron bars, that were driven down deep into it. The rough door handle protrudes in a half circle and, to open it, you must give it a good, hard tug, weight back on your heels. There is a noise in my Room of Doom and Gloom, it's from the show Donnie Darko. One song that loops is The Tangent Universe. Google it and you'll feel the dark and cold in this room.

But there is light in it too, and when I am dealing with a

painful memory, I can summon a brilliant light to illuminate the appropriate scene, that I've created each time I've needed relief. There is a nightstand with an empty bottle of red wine and glass with barely a sip left. Lying next to the pair is a couple OxyContin. But with the light on, it's not so scary, embarrassing, or shameful. It's just a memory and I know that I'm better for it, that I can't change what's happened, but I can accept and learn. I make up that if I had not had that experience, I could have had a much worse one, perhaps becoming addicted when my doctor gave a prescription for 30 of them after a surgery with two refills! Twenty-five were trashed, despite a friend telling me I could 'sell them for some serious cash.' Really?

My word 'fun' has also helped me be lighter about that situation. Now, when I retell that story, I get a bit tickled at the ridiculousness of what I did. I also know I learned from it, just like we all can from every experience. And, being willing to recount it, owning my mistake and shame, gives it less power over me. I know I did not intend to upset or insult anyone and their inability to give me what I needed, an awareness of who I was (not someone who intends to wound) and sincere forgiveness, does not mean I did not deserve it. So, I gave it to myself and let it go, revisiting it only as a ridiculous event that, perhaps, kept me from becoming a statistic.

Here's an idea, imagine what your room of doom and gloom would look like, smell like, feel like and add as many features as possible that come to you by writing in your journal. Think about how'd you enter the room and if there are sounds or a terrible kind of silence. Use your imagination and then think about a memory that causes you shame, pain, guilt, sadness, distraction and put it there. Create the memory in a medium you like, a moving picture, a still shot, a painting, sculpture, or song. Then let the light shine on it. Imagine some stadium-level lights are illuminating the scene that brings you pain or sorrow. Let it exist and feel its power over you wane. This room is always available to you, but when you visit it, when you read your journal, the section that has some hard stories in it, you will leave lighter and hopeful, forgiving yourself with a fuller understanding that it is from our mistakes that we grow.

As I've given workshops, I've learned so much from the attendees. They wow me with their creativity and stories and willingness to step into discomfort. When I explain the room of doom and gloom, I share that the idea came to be when a friend told me about having to deliver a baby who had died in utero at 8+ months. I thought, if that had happened to me, I'd be frozen and depressed. I couldn't imagine moving on. How had she done that, and continued to find joy?

She said that a few weeks after she had lost the baby, she had been driving down Hillsboro Pike at Christmas time in south Nashville. The Christmas tree-filled front of Hillsboro High School was full of families, kids squealing as they played hide and seek among the mini-forest, fire pits glowing. As she noticed the happy scene from her car, she had an epiphany, that despite the awfulness of her experience, she could move on from it. She could honor that it had happened but not be controlled or defined by it. And just like that she did. When she told me that story, the idea of having a place to put bad experiences, the room of doom and gloom, came to me.

My hope is that you will take some time to reflect on any experiences that are causing you grief or pain, feelings of 'less than' or shame and let them sit in your imaginary room of doom and gloom, where the light will illuminate them, take them out of the shadows and create, instead of dread, a list of learnings that serve you. In my room, there is an old-fashioned scroll, where I can read all that I have learned from bad experiences, close calls and straight up stupidity. Put pen to paper in your journal and write as much as feels comfortable to you about an experience that brings you discomfort.

◆ ◆ ◆

Take time to identify any mistakes, sad events any experiences that weigh on you and acknowledge them by journaling about or drawing. Shine a light on things that weigh on you by journaling and accepting they happened and you will experience relief as their power over you dissipates.

◆ ◆ ◆

A college student shared with me that she started by just writing down a date; more than that was too much at first. But after a few weeks of journaling about more upbeat experiences and thinking about her wishes and dreams, she was able to add more details to the date. Then she wrote 'the thing that happened'. She did not write what happened, but just those words, 'the thing that happened' and the date. It took her months but then she said it just all came flying out and she wrote pages and pages with illustrations of her negative experience. When she asked me if I'd meet her for a walk at Centennial Park and told me that, I was moved beyond words. I did not ask her for the details, and she chose to keep them to herself, but what she told me was that she'd never felt more hopeful and free, that she had come out of a depression she did not realize she was in…by journaling.

Coulda, Woulda, Shoulda

I imagine and journal about a passageway between my metaphorical room of happiness and gloom and doom. It leads to a small holding area. Sometimes a memory I place into my room of happiness begins to morph into something that does not serve me or from which I need to learn. That happens with age or reflection; I have, for example, re-read my description of an event from my early 20s, only to think more deeply about it and realize that the experience was more of a learning one and might need to make a move from my room of happiness into a place of learning and reflection: almost got a DUI; slept in airport because I didn't have money for a hotel room; tore up my ankle after falling from the back of the couch on which I was dancing; feigned having to go to the bathroom, being surrounded by a group of men in Tunisia City (didn't understand middle eastern culture), crawling out a restaurant window to escape the guy who gave me the heebie-jeebies and kept asking me if I wanted to have another drink, that he'd get. No thanks.

Despite the fun in the moment, or with the excitement of retelling the story, with time, I have realized some of these experiences were near misses and examples of how important it is to listen to our inner voices. By reflecting on them, I learn a lot. I don't get bogged down in what almost happened, but instead, form a strong memory about what prevented something negative from happening, namely, listening to my instincts!

Here is one such memory, a 'could have happened' moment..

The kids were 6 months, 2 and 3 years old I had decided to take them to Waffle House for 'breakfast for dinner' one weekend when my husband was out of town. After enjoying some scattered, covered, smothered, and diced hashbrowns and pancakes, I gathered up my gaggle of kids and headed to the car. As soon as I was out of the restaurant, the hair on the back of my neck stood up and I turned to see two men approaching. It was not to offer to help me.

The one in front and I locked eyes and I froze, knowing I was, at best, about to be robbed. I thought, "shit, I have no cash and that's going to piss them off". So, I asked for what I wanted.

"Hey man." I said guiding the toddlers behind me, while my infant daughter dangled in a car seat hooked in my elbow. "Can I please have a pass? I have my kids with me."

And he stopped, hesitated, put his arm out, stopping the forward movement of him and his partner, and said, "Ok". Then he turned around and headed the other direction. I opened the driver's side door and scooted the boys and then my infant daughter in the car seat in, wiggled in behind them and locked the doors.

"What did those people want?" asked my 3-year-old.

"I don't know for sure. But whatever it was, they changed their minds." was my response.

That scene could have unfolded so differently. But it didn't. I learned a couple of lessons that evening. First, check out your surroundings a bit more diligently and second, ask for what you want. Sometimes, you'll get it.

Asking for help is not something I'm wired to do naturally. In fact, my tendency, my initial reaction is to do things on my own. A yoga instructor once said 'we control things we don't trust' and at times that's why I do things instead of asking others to, because whatever the thing is, is important to me and I don't trust someone else to get it done. There. I said it. When something is very important to me my initial reaction is to do it myself because I've had impactful experiences that influenced my assumptions. I assume that the best odds are when I do the thing. But is that a fact?

To improve my tendency to ask for help has required me to be more thoughtful and intentional about doing so. I started small by letting a fellow passenger get my suitcase out of the overhead for me. I am completely capable of doing that and often help others when getting off a plane, but, until I began to think about it, wouldn't consider letting someone help me – a bit crazy, right? Nope – it's not crazy, it's that we form habits and don't always take time to consider the why behind them.

As a young woman and later as a woman business owner, I learned early that asking for help was a weakness, so, I think, developed a pattern of not asking. I imagine now any therapist reading this would enjoy going deep on that one. Now that I'm aware of my tendency to fly solo, I see it more often and can choose to give someone the gift of helping. We try to control what we don't trust. Journal about what you tend to control and let the insights begin!

◆ ◆ ◆

Ask for what you want. Ask your bank, your clients, your co-workers, a stranger. The odds are zero that you'll get a positive response when you don't ask the question.

Intersections

Thank you for reading about The Three Words and for starting to journal your stories in each area. The next section, *Intersections*, are my stories about how my three words and life experiences blend. My hope is that you will start journaling about your three words and think about your stories that are related to them. Ask older relatives to share their memories of pictures from your youth and write it all down. See if you can find intersections between the stories that interest you the most and your words. By looking for intersections and journaling about them, I have learned more about how I am wired and what experiences will feed my positive words more than my shadow ones. I hope that you will learn more and write more and embrace who you are, well, more.

Fit

In the mid 70's my dad started running. Jim Fixx had written a book 'The Complete Book of Running' that had been part of a running revolution. One morning my dad stumbled back into the house, wearing shorty shorts, no shirt with a washcloth tucked into the waist band. He was breathing hard, and sweat was dripping from his chin and chest hair, ah, parents.

"Guess what I just did!" he gasped.

My brothers and I looked up from our cereal and waited for him to tell us.

"I just ran 2 miles!" He crowed. He was jubilant!

We were sincerely impressed. And that's how it began. I started running. Usually, I ran by myself and learned to eke through the discomfort of that first mile, to push through to the top of a hill and feel the quiet pride of not stopping when the urge to do so was mighty and there was no one around to see.

Occasionally Dad and I would run together, and I began to associate running with a father's love. He would let me talk about whatever was on my mind and include me in discussions, when, on occasion, I joined his friends for a run. Those runs felt very grown up.

On a run during my 15th year, we were about 2 miles in to 8 when he said:

"You know, Beck, sometimes a long, slow run can help with premenstrual and menstrual cramps." I looked for a rock to crawl under and tried to muster an instant ability to be invisible.

But with hindsight I appreciated that he was willing to discuss absolutely anything with me.

We had running stories to share: the time (pre-cell phones) we got caught in a rainstorm 5 miles out in Memphis and had to run back, our cotton track suits getting heavier and heavier. The dogs that almost got us. This uphill or that epic downhill. Running brought us closer and, I believe, fed right into the energy I got from feeling fit.

I was never a fast runner, although I fantasized about being one. I could go far, say 8-10 miles, but it was more like a slog than the long-legged, floating form I imagined.

As an 8th grader, my French teacher, Mrs. Pruitt invited me to run the first all-women race, The Bonnie Belle 10k. It was in spring and felt so full of great energy to be one of several thousand girls and women standing on Legislative Plaza milling about with other fit females. That experience also, I believe, gave me more clarity about my desire to be inclusive and equitable. These were the pre-title IX days, or at least TN hadn't fully adopted them yet, so I had experienced not being allowed to do a lot of things that the young boys and men were encouraged and supported to do. I just wanted to be able to try out for the baseball team, not be told 'no' because of my gender.

Once in high school, I ran track and cross country, my enthusiasm making up for my lack of talent, and I won the coach's award for best attitude as I laughed and encouraged my talented teammates, truly reveling in their skill and achievements. My fit and fun words were appearing and taking more space than others. A teetotaler more often than not, in high school I was regularly and happily the designated driver, after arriving to one early-morning cross country meet hungover, I vowed never to do that again. Running, then, as I got older hiking, biking and walking, less pounding activities, are examples of where my fit, fun and focus all intersect.

When we find those areas of intersection, it's blissful. Creating natural intersections is something we can do with a little intention. If you spend some time thinking about the stories related to each of your three words, you will find why or when those words became important and meaningful to you.

My friend, Rod, shared that he had invited a friend to come with him to Alaska. Rod had been a guide there for years and his friend had received a scary cancer diagnosis. He wanted to experience Alaska while he could. They flew one of those water-landing planes in and spent a week without seeing another person, just enjoying nature and peace. I had met with Rod just before he left for that trip and saw him again 2 days after he returned. He had this calm about him, like he'd had a week of the best sleep ever. Nurture (one of his words) had wrapped them both in a blanket of peace.

◆ ◆ ◆

Find ways to live your three words and have experiences that strengthen them. Think about times in your past where those intersections have happened and journal about them.

Fit Me Introduced Me To
Courageous Me

On Tuesday nights in my youth, my parents left my brothers and me alone for the evening while they went to rehearsal with The Nashville Symphony Chorus. We loved it. We got to eat tv dinners and do whatever we wanted.

I practiced gymnastics at First Presbyterian church, a few minutes' walk from my house on Robertson Academy. On this normal, summer, Tuesday evening, I was walking my regular route back through the side field next to the horse pasture. As I approached the thick hedge between the field and my neighbor's back yard, I saw one of the neighborhood boys and my brother's friend, Brad. I don't remember exactly what happened but suddenly, he was on top of me tugging at my shorts. I had absolutely no idea what he was doing. I shoved him off of me and stood up over him and kicked him in the nuts as hard as I could with my red, leather, pointed cowboy boots and ran home.

When I told my older brother, Stuart what had happened he told me to stay there. I make up that I imagined some of this, but what I remember is that he came home a few minutes later with blood on his knuckles and told me that 'Brad will never touch you again'. I believed him.

Then he got serious.
"Look, Beck, we gotta keep this secret. If Mom and Dad find out, it'll ruin Tuesday nights."

I happily agreed, thinking that I did not want to lose that Tuesday-night freedom either. I flipped on Starsky and Hutch as I munched on my Salisbury Steak TV dinner, not only unphased but jacked up with 'you won't mess with me and my smokin' hot pointy red cowboy boots, they or my big brother will dominate'.

Thinking back on that moment, it could have gone so differently. At 9 or 10, I didn't know what rape was. I reacted with the instinct of a girl raised with two brothers. They fight, you fight back. I wasn't scared, I was mad. Had Brad overpowered and raped me, I imagine things might have turned out a lot differently for me. Maybe I would have told my parents and gotten counseling and been ok, but maybe I would have, like many girls and women do, thought I was somehow to blame. Maybe I would have become distant and depressed, my parents unable to figure out what was going on. Maybe I would have started self-soothing with drugs or alcohol.

Instead, I was introduced to courageous me, and that courage didn't make me mean or an irresponsible risk taker; it made me comfortable in discomfort, because I believed (in that moment) that I could get out of any situation. As I got older, I gained some discernment and with experience knew when to avoid a situation as the courageous act and when to listen to fear when it was warning me about real danger. I found out much later in life that Brad had been regularly beaten and threatened by his father. He and his older brother both died of drug overdoses in their 30s or 40s. Hurt people hurt people.

I learned to be comfortable walking away when things got too heated or talking people off the ledge. I learned to call people out privately, not in a group setting, if there was any chance they would see and change the error of their constant rambling, racist or sexist comments. Public shaming never worked. I was drawn to situations that would test and teach me and left each one a better version of myself, not needing to share, brag or boast but wanting to think about what I learned and how I could use it to be a better person. The results, a success or failure, became less and less important than the experience and what I learned. When I stopped keeping score, my willingness to try new things, especially those that intimidated me, only grew.

I think that my 'fit' word got its strength partially due to how that situation, being attacked on a walk home, played out. My child mind told me that my physical strength, my fitness level, is what saved me. In my 50s , I'm very aware of how luck and good fortune have impacted by life. At that age, I didn't think for a second that luck had played a part. I was already embracing fitness in gymnastics, running with my Dad, and was inspired by the Olympic gymnasts and runners like Mary Decker. With hindsight, I believe I was looking for, that I needed to see, women who were athletic champions, because my young brain, told me that it was my athleticism that saved me.

◆ ◆ ◆

Think about pivotal events in your life that inspired you, helped your words find power and give those events and words space to exist in your journal and psyche.

Giving Back

Becca Stevens started Thistle Farms in the mid '90s. When I heard about it in the early 2000s, I immediately got involved, volunteering when they started making candles at a church on Vanderbilt's campus. I copied this from their website (https://thistlefarms.org/):

> "*After experiencing the death of her father and subsequent child abuse when she was 5, Becca Stevens longed to open a sanctuary for survivors offering a loving community. In 1997, Becca opened our first home as a sanctuary for 5 women survivors.*
>
> *Four years later, the women were making great strides in recovery, but struggling to become financially self-sufficient due to employment barriers.*
>
> *To address this, Becca, volunteers, and residents began making candles in a church basement and, in 2001, Thistle Farms social enterprises were born.*"

After I bought my first business, in 2002, I hired several women going through the Thistle Farms program to help open the bins and bins of mail we would receive during our busy season, before there was a digital way to receive things! We would all sit around a large table slicing open envelopes, sorting, and stacking and chatting. I thought it was great and was unphased that all of them had worked as prostitutes and often had experienced drug addiction.

But my feelings did not align with my permanent co-workers. At the end of one day, one of my full-time employees walked into my office looking a bit sheepish, but also pissed off. I changed her name for this book:

"Becky, can we talk about, uh, the ladies you hired to help open the mail?"

"Sure."

"Today, one of them told me she was hungry."

"Oh. I can get some extra stuff for the kitchen on my way in tomorrow." I offered.

"No, I mean, ok, but what I mean is, do you think it's a good idea to have those kind of people in here?"

I could feel my neck heating up and my toes curling under.

"Those kind of people?" I said, mad.

"You know. I mean. They are all…"

She didn't finish the sentence; I imagine because she could see my anger. We just stared at each other for a second, neither one of us wanting to escalate. She was in a precarious position. I signed her paycheck and, she knew now, had a very different mindset regarding 'those people'. She started to turn and leave, and I stopped her.

"Anita, I appreciate you being honest with me and I'm sorry I did something that made you, or anyone uncomfortable."

She smiled.

"Can you give me until tomorrow to think about this?"

"Sure." Was her response. She meant it.

On the way home I called my mentor, Tim, and told him about it. As usual, he had great advice and some chastising. "You need to go get your volunteering needs, your charitable needs, met out of the office. Look, Becky, not everyone is going to find it professional or even comfortable working with former prostitutes."

I argued, but I knew he was right. The message that my people had gotten, despite it not being mine, was that the job we did, opening the mail in the busy season, could be done by people without a deep skill set. It made them feel like they were doing something beneath them. I was furious and I fantasized, briefly, about firing everyone, and hiring only women from Thistle Farms.

I didn't think any job was beneath me. Sure, I have had jobs I liked better than others, but I had been raised to believe that all honest work was worthy of doing with pride. My people were not able to process that positively. I had an ah-ha and my hands gripped my steering wheel in anger as Tim shined a bright light on who was at the center of all this dysfunction; it was me.

I had not hired any of my co-workers - they had all been with the company when I bought it - so I had kept them on. I had not reassessed my workforce, had not had them re-interview for their jobs, or been very specific about what was going to change and how success would be measured by position.

I don't think anyone is better than anyone else, but I understood his point, that asking my people to work alongside those ladies, had made them feel like I was saying the job at hand could be done by people they viewed as less than, implying I thought they were less than. Also, I had not included them in the decision, first exposing them to Becca and the program. I had, naively, assumed that if I liked the idea they would too. I make all of these statements as though I know what was in the mind of my employees. After all of this passed, I talked with them and what I shared came from what they told me about how they felt.

It was a hard conversation, and I was mad and disappointed, but Tim was right. I was running a business not social enterprise like

Becca was. He was also right that I needed to give back and help.

I needed to get those needs met outside of the office. I also wanted the business to give back; thanks to Tim's insights, I asked my co-workers to pick local charities they wanted to support and I started volunteering on my own time.

Tim also pointed out that I 'seemed to be hiring people who needed rescuing, instead of people who are smarter and faster than you'. Defensive at first, I reminded him I had inherited all of them. I could hear the disappointment in his voice to my adolescent response.
"Come on Becky, you know what I mean."
I did, damn it.

I knew I had some serious work to do. He was right; the majority of my staff were mediocre at best, putting me at high risk of losing the A players. I had created an environment where it appeared that I was the only A player, fully evolved, the be all end all, and that was very far from the truth.

It felt good to have all the answers to be the person they all came to. I knew what I really wanted was to be challenged, be around people who had skills I would never master and from whom I could learn. I had stepped into the victim-villain-hero triangle. Was nicely ensconced in it, getting hero needs met day-after-day. Realizing this disgusted me. I felt like I had been wasting time, acting like the competent pilot and co-pilot, when, in reality, in my business life, I was not flying, I was safely coming and going from a simulator.

So, with A LOT of Tim's help, I started analyzing who my next hire needed to be. First, we identified things I was doing at which I was not good and that I did not really enjoy doing. The detail-oriented things were the first: payroll and technology. And thus, a delegation campaign began. As I delegated tasks at which I was not stellar or ones I did not really enjoy, they were completed more efficiently and with fewer errors. I found myself with more time to think about the big picture, the long term, which was exactly where I found my spark, my energy.

◆ ◆ ◆

Give back in your community. Seek out not-for-profits that align with you core values or three words. You'll know you've chosen wisely, when you feel energized, not drained when you volunteer.

Delegate what you're not great at and what you don't love doing to people who are better than you.

◆ ◆ ◆

Some people saw the writing on the wall and tried to cajole me to slow down and 'do things like we used to'. One particularly humorous exchange was about a tradition the former owner had started of keeping the office fridge full of lunch supplies: meat, cheese, condiments, and bread for sandwiches. He had done this to reduce the amount of time people spent going out to lunch but sold it to the team as a benefit: we cover your lunch!

I had kept it going for a couple of years, but, with my new focus on running a business, not a high school, I had regularly thought about how to end it without a revolt that would, ultimately, hurt our clients, if people left without a trained replacement.

Tim had told me to 'rip off the band aid' several times. I had been avoiding doing so until Marissa told me she'd be in late (again) 'tomorrow'.

"Becky, I've got to stop by Kroger to restock the fridge on my way in tomorrow, so will be in late." Marissa said.

"I'll pick up the groceries." I responded, without thinking about it, again, the back of my neck warming up as I felt anger coming on.

"Oh, no, I like doing it. It's ok. I got it." She insisted.

"Nope. I'm going to handle the groceries for this week and then we will no longer be covering lunch supplies." I was standing firm.

"Why?" she whined. She was not happy.

"Because I don't want to do this anymore. I'm tired of picking up groceries being a reason for coming in late."

Her face was bright red, and I was, I'll admit, impressed, when she raised her voice. Really yelling – about groceries.

"But Nyles (the former owner) said he would pay for our lunches!"

"Yes, he did. And I'm changing that policy."

"Are you going to give us a pay raise to cover the difference?" Man, was she pushing it.

I think, with a bit of intended drama, I let my head fall and exhaled.

"No. I am going to expect everyone to act like adults and accept the change." She huffed out and I heard her go into a co-worker's office, slam the door and begin to yell.

I walked into that office and they both looked up. I felt like I was evolving in the moment. I suddenly knew that I needed to be very clear about what I intended. I felt a cool calm surround me, felt very much at peace.

"Look, ladies, I am not going to allow yelling, pouting, gossiping or any other non-adult behavior. If you choose to act that way, you'll be expected to resign or you'll be fired. I'm done with this type of behavior."

Marissa, still livid, kept her mouth shut, but within a month was fired after she was caught lying to a client and then lying about lying. It took 2 years, but at the end of that time all but 1 of the original team had left or been fired. It was a new time, but one still fraught with my missteps and assumptions.

◆ ◆ ◆

Hire, coach and fire according to your core values. All behavior you allow shows your standards and what you view as acceptable.

Fit and Fun meet Focused

When you are aware of your three words (and their shadows) you will begin to notice intersections and potential pitfalls that will benefit from your attention. My brother, C.R., told me about being a volunteer, in NYC, with Achilles International, an organization that pairs able-bodied athletes with athletes who are blind or have another physical challenges so that they can participate in athletics. I signed up with the Nashville chapter and at one evening practice an organizer with Achilles asked me if I would help an athlete train for a 5k.

"Sure." Was my quick response.

"Wait, before you agree.", she cautioned. "He and his wife are blind and getting to group training sessions is tough for them. He is looking for someone who will come to his house and run from there a few times a week."

"Sure." I repeated. I was in. At that point in time, I had trained with and completed several runs or races with Achilles athletes and I understood, well, let's say I had been exposed to, not that I really understood their dilemma and struggle with something I found effortless: lacing up my Asics and going for a jog. All I had to do was muster the motivation. These athletes depended on someone to be available, capable of guiding a blind person and able to move at the desired pace for the desired distance.
I was going to make training with Joe a priority.

After a couple phone calls and text exchanges we had a Tuesday-Thursday-Saturday routine confirmed. The drive to his place in Madison from mine was about 30 minutes. I'd drive 30, jog 30, drive 30, three times a week. I felt elated, like I had been given this special assignment.

The first afternoon that I showed up, I came straight from work and needed to change into my running gear. Joe and his wife, Lisa, lived on the ground floor of an apartment complex. When I pulled up, he was standing outside of their door, ready to go.

"Can I run in and change my clothes?" I asked.

"You can change right here if you want, it's not like I'm going to see anything." He joked.

I laughed. "You and I, my friend, are going to get along just fine." He was telling blind jokes already. I could not wait to hear his story. I could feel the positive energy that comes when someone's work (fun) and mine align.

As I walked into the apartment he said, "watch out for that one." gesturing to a precious little girl who looked to be about 3.

"She has figured out that we can't see and has a wicked sense of humor. She's learned how to move things around so that we trip over them and regularly pushes an ottoman or chair to the middle of the room and waits like a hyena until we take a fall and then cackles loudly. I'm going to break my neck!"

"What?" I ask, stunned.

"Oh yeah. She is pure evil." he laughed.

"Get this, last week, she found our cell phones, silenced them, and hid them under our mattress. It took us days to find them. I'm thinking about tying her up." He joked. He was impressed and not at all bitter. Like all parents, he was just trying to figure out how to parent.

"I'll be right back." I told him as I closed the bathroom door to change my clothes. The bathroom was tidy and smelled particularly fresh. But the corners were filthy with that black mildew that accumulates. I closed my eyes: clean, nice. I opened them: someone's slacking on the detail work.

As I pulled on my shoes and gathered my work clothes, shoving them into a Kroger bag I'd brought, I thought how in the hell do you raise kids if you can't see?

When I emerged, I heard Joe's voice from the kitchen and walked in. His wife Lisa was mixing hamburger meat in a bowl.

"It's meatloaf night!" He said enthusiastically.

Lisa turned and said hi. Her 8 month+ pregnant belly protruding beautifully.

"When are you due?"

Joe interrupted. "She's not pregnant, she just really likes Doritos."

This guy.

"Shut up, honey. Hi Becky. Thank you for running with Joe. I'm due in 5 weeks. It's another girl."

"Congrats!"

Joe jumped in: "And then I'm gonna get the snip, snip.', Joe shared. 'Man-to-man coverage has been bad enough. Zone is gonna be a bitch!" his eyes glistening.

"I have a question, Lisa. How do you keep up with what's in the fridge?"

Lisa explained their system and I thought about that scene in the movie, Minority Report, when Tom Cruise wakes up from eyeball replacement surgery, starving and goes to the fridge to grab a sandwich. There is one good one and about a dozen rotten ones. But he can't see because his eyes are bandaged. He grabs a bad on and starts snarfing it down, only to have to spit it out, realizing it's putrid.

I'd starve if I were blind, I thought, and, I didn't think I had the courage to raise kids without the benefit of sight. I felt like I was in the presence of some superheroes, people with skills unimaginable, unattainable to me.

"One more question before we head out. How do you, well, keep up with a baby?"

"Thanks for asking." Lisa said, turning from her bowl and leaning against the kitchen counter. "Lots of people go straight to 'blind people shouldn't have kids. I appreciate that you're interested. Basically, we have to keep a hand on it at all times."

"That's what she said!" crowed Joe. "You have to say, you set that up, babe."

"Enough!" Said Lisa. "Y'all go run. And Becky, I'm sorry."

"Sorry?" I asked, concerned for a second that I had said something insensitive.

"Yeah.", she said giggling, "now you get to endure him!"

Joe and I trained for several weeks. And during that time, he told me his story. He had gone blind in high school, an inherited disease. For 'several years' he was bitter and spent most of his time, according to him, lashing out at anyone and everything, drinking and doing drugs, being reckless. He said, 'I was in full on victim mode for about 5 years.' Then, he told me, he finally accepted things and began to mellow. He joined a community of blind people. Began to feel less alone. He learned how to manage vending machines, started installing them, making money, feeling independent and life got better. He started finding humor in his situation.

When he heard about Achilles, he was especially excited. He had played football until he lost his sight and loved anything athletic.

One day, before a training run, he asked me to wait a sec while he finished up something with his 7-year-old son, who was sitting in front of a computer. The kid had on thick glasses that were secured with an elastic band. Joe was guiding his son's hand. When I peeked down at the paper, I noticed it was braille. On our run I asked him about it.

"He has the same eye disease I do." Joe told me bluntly. "I'm teaching him braille now so that when he goes blind, he'll be way ahead of the curve."

Holy shit. My child rearing challenges got a lot smaller in that moment.

The day of our race I picked Joe up and we drove to the event. It was a Warrior Dash: mud, obstacles, fire pits. Joe was excited and bouncy. It was a beautiful fall day: blue skies, cool but not cold. We ran a mile and then encountered the first obstacle: a ditch under barbed wire.

"Keep your butt very low" was my instruction. We breezed through it, dirtiness the only major result.

Then there was a rope wall to climb and Joe scurred up it like a spider. I had to hustle to keep up.

The 4-inch balance beam over a 6-foot fall to a bunch of huge rocks, made a lump form in my throat as I imagined us in a heap, bones protruding.

"Ok, so there is a very narrow beam we've got to cross. One foot in front of the other and slow, ok?"

"How far is the fall?" Joe queried.

"I'll tell you on the other side. Imagine it's a foot."

So, sharing a tether, I on the left and he on the right, we walked across it. Dismounting he said, "that was about 6 feet up wasn't it?"

"Yep and you crushed it. I said, genuinely impressed and very much relieved.

Joe whooped and I joined him. With less than a ½ mile to go I could see the smoke.

"There's some sort of fire thing coming up." I offered.

"A little more detail would be appreciated, slacker guide." Joe added, grinning.

As we got close, I could see the flames and wondered what all had been included in the release we'd signed. How did these races get insurance?
"Ok, so there is a fire and we're supposed to jump over it. There is a path around it, so if you don't want to jump, we can take the detour."

"Are you kidding? We are jumping." Joe shouted, picking up the pace and pulling me a bit.

"Hey, now, I'm the guide." I reminded him, taking up the slack and settling in on his left, slightly ahead of him.

"Ok, then, when I say 'jump' you need to jump up AND forward. You need to clear about 4 feet to avoid landing in the fire pit. And we need to jump at the same time on my count."

We picked up the pace and I described our approach. "We are 20 yards out, now 15, now 10. When I get to one we jump. 5-4-3-2-1 JUMP!!!"

◆ ◆ ◆

Take time to evaluate your biases and what influences them. Is it how someone looks or talks?

How would you react if you experienced someone without the benefit of sight or hearing?

What I did not know was that someone snapped a picture of that moment. Like many stories I relate, some people think I'm making stuff up or exaggerating. I love that picture. Joe is all in. Feet tucked, trusting that I've told him what he needs to know to avoid LANDING IN A FIRE PIT. We both are so in the moment, focused. It's a moment I treasure and one that taught me the impact of surrendering, trusting, deciding to make the best out of whatever life throws at you, of embracing a positive mindset. Thanks, Joe. You are, for sure, not a slacker. You are a guide and a co-pilot and was a part of one of those incredible intersecting moments. My fun and fitness merged with focused and for a moment it was all that was.

"We don't stop playing because we grow old; we grow old because we stop playing." - George Bernard Shaw

In the previous intersections, I shared some of my stories that are meant to help you begin to think about which stories you tend to re-tell, which memories come back most often and what theme or words are in them. As you start journaling, you might recall more of the stories in your life and see the patterns in their themes.

Legacy

What would you like your legacy to be? How would you like to be remembered? What would that look like? For what do you want to be remembered? What are some words that come to mind?

My Legacy Words are:

1. Motivating
2. Magnanimous
3. Devoted

If I had to pick one, it would be magnanimous, which is defined as 'generous or forgiving, especially toward a rival or less powerful person.' I am very energized to work on being so. And, by journaling about it, I find that not only have my actions improved but, over time, even my thoughts have become more gracious and kind towards people whose beliefs and views are very different from mine.

What's a word that describes how you want to be remembered?

I wish I had a diary that a great, great relative had written a hundred years before I was born in which they told me what mattered, what lessons they had learned and what mistakes they had made, wanting me to do and be better.

When I write to my great, great, great, I just share what's going on with an occasional lesson. Mostly I want them to know what I experienced and for them to draw their own conclusions. Maybe they'll find me silly or old fashioned. The more I journal, the more I find that I can pause before making a decision, acting or saying something and think 'is this what I'd want my great-great-great to know I did or said?'

Thinking about this future relative, who I will never know, helps be a better person, to live my legacy word more often than not. It's a stretch to be generous or forgiving towards a rival. The part, being generous or forgiving towards a less powerful person, comes easily to me. But my competitive side often encourages me to be less so with someone I consider a rival, especially when my righteousness activates and I view my philosophy, politics and views to be correct and theirs wrong, or in the worst case invalid.

One way to become more conscious of what's important to you, in addition to coming up with your legacy word, is to journal about what you'd do if you had 24 hours to live. If you could go anywhere and do anything with anyone, what would you do?

I've never heard someone say they would be rude to a waitress or display road rage in their last hours. In general, people want to spend time with the people they love. They want to experience something on their bucket list; they want to live their legacy.

So, in closing, I'd like you to journal about how you would spend your last day and why you picked certain people and activities and not others. Ask yourself this question: how and with whom am I spending time now and how would that change if I knew I had a day to live? Sure, we all have to go to the grocery store and do the mundane tasks, but are we doing them with a positive, grateful mindset or a negative, fussy one?

When we take time to imagine how we would act and think if our time were short, we learn how to shift our mindsets to be more positive and appreciative.

◆ ◆ ◆

Make a LONG dream list of everything you'd like to experience, do, have and be. Then think about what you can experience now. Don't wait. Live your legacy.

CONCLUSION

Conclusion

I hope thinking about your three words, their shadows, and your legacy word has helped you think more deeply about why they are your words. I also hope that you are now more motivated to write about your experiences in and with them. I encourage you to share these stories with people you love and trust and have wonderful conversations spurred on from your sharing.

I have heard so many incredible stories from people and the gravy is when they let me know how journaling made them more aware of what was lingering in their subconscious, waiting to be released. That release can bring joy or sadness, but either way, it is release, that results in more mental space to grow and evolve, and evolve requires love, both grammatically and experientially.

When the draft of this book was complete, I asked my parents to read it. My father, whose eyes tired easily suggested I read it to him, and the result was a memory for my room of happiness, a journal entry I'll share to close:

It's a gray February day and Dad has the fireplace on. Whenever I see his gas fireplace it makes me giggle a bit because, growing up, I experienced him cutting our wood and heating the house with a fireplace. He would have scoffed at a gas fireplace, implying they were for lazy, wasteful people. He's evolved to enjoy and appreciate the easy warmth of fake logs and a remote controlled off-on switch.

He's also evolved in terms of his relationships with cats. My brothers and I get a regular belly laugh when one of brings up our father's devotion to felines. He's now had 4 or 5, the most recent being the ones that crack us up the most - they are Himalayans, fussy, high-maintenance types. Growing up we were raised by the 'we don't need to fix the dogs' type for whom cats were not considered a potential family pet, but a python was.

So, as I sit with my 87-year old Dad in front of the gas fire with his fancy cats, I am in a silly mood. I start reading from the introduction and we spend the next two hours with him listening intently, making suggestions, asking questions, and helping me rephrase something. When we get to the story of why one of my words is 'fit', I choke up a bit while reading it and his eyes tear up and he says 'I only wish I could run with you now'. And I say, 'you did when it mattered and maybe another word is beginning to come to the surface because of what we are doing right now. I feel like my words will also evolve and that 'write' might need to be added to my list. Maybe there are more than just three words.'

My Dad winked at me and says: 'there are a lot more than three, honey, a lot more.'

◆ ◆ ◆

I hope you start journaling about your words and their related stories so that you can get to know yourself better and can, thus, spend more time doing things and being with people who feed you at your best. At the beginning of this book I shared an image with 'You' in the middle, surrounded by your three words, your shadow words, your stories and your legacy. I hope you take time to think more deeply about each area so that you learn to recognize which your choices are energizing. And, it is my wish that you will use journaling to explore who you are and what matters to you. If, in 100 years, a great, great relative finds your journal, what will you want them to learn from your stories and how will you want them to describe you? Write you'll legacy and you'll live it.

The End.

Epilogue

I'm sitting in an airport lounge in Sao Paula, a city I've never visited, on the way back from Mendoza, Argentina where my husband, Michael and I just spent a week as a part of a Sister Cities program. While there, we talked a lot about the extreme privilege we, and many Americans have, and to us, seem to take for granted, not really notice.

I think the not noticing part is due largely to what I started calling, on this trip, 'the size of peoples' bubbles'. If your bubble of people and experiences is small, it's easy to get around in yours without much effort. When we take the same route to the same grocery store and buy the same things and hang out with the same people, our bubbles stay small, familiar and very manageable.

I'm trying to be intentional about pushing my bubble to grow, getting to know people who are very different from me, trying new things, analyzing my habits to determine if they are encouraging me to stretch or settle for familiar and safe. At a salad bar or buffet, do I always choose the same thing? On this trip, we met a couple who had never travelled internationally. At the end of the first day, when we had some free time, Michael and I wandered around, found a local restaurant and managed, over a few laughs and a lot of patience from the Mendozans, to get pretty much what we thought we were ordering. On the way home we got a text from the couple asking about the currency exchange rate and how to find a place for dinner. By the time we got the message it was late and they were already in bed. Instead of exploring they had stayed in their room, too nervous, they told us, to, well, expand their circle.

I don't know what their life experiences have been; don't know where their nervousness came from, but did let them know that we were very comfortable wandering around and they were welcome to join us, which they did; slowly, over a few days they ventured out more and more, ending the week with a smile and a waive from across a plaza as they headed out to do some shopping – voila!, circles expanded.

And so, with that experience came the idea for my next book: Big bubble, little bubbles: how diversity of experience and relationships will make you smarter, enhance your life and help you change habits that aren't serving you. Here's the first chapter:

COMING SOON

Chapter One

Arugula

In the mid-1990s, Michael and I went to dinner for a special occasion at Zola's, one of Nashville's first gourmet restaurants. At the recommendation of the waiter, we both ordered the French Laundry salad.

'What kind of lettuce is this?' we asked each other.

The waiter told us it was arugula.

Huh. Peppery, tangy, long leaves. We were hooked.

Nowadays you can get it a Wal-Mart; but back then it was hard to find. I bought some seeds and started growing our own and was rewarded with bundles of fresh greens 6-7 months of the year.

Then on trip to Italy a pizza came with a pile of it and we were delighted by the cool of it combined with the heat and crunch of the pizza – just wow! Our kids grew up thinking pizza is always served with a bunch of arugula on top. We've tried to parent them to be curious, big bubble people, not giving in to the pressure, for example, of feeding them something different than we ate at a meal. They grew up thinking sushi and arugula was on every kid's menu, that all kitchens had a nice, thick Italian balsamic in the pantry.

Our minds expand as we open ourselves up to new experiences. Instead of saying 'I don't eat...whatever, we are curious and delighted with a new flavor. In my experience, all people like yummy and it's rare that something offered is not exactly that. Dairy products and I don't get along, so I have to be careful, but being pescatarian is a choice, so sometimes I fall off the wagon and try something new, especially if it's a local favorite. Just a taste, a bite of something can tell you a lot about the local culture. Spicy. Not spicy. Lots of salt. No cinnamon (thanks, France), hot chicken (thanks Nashville), not quite dead (no thanks, Korea).

In Mendoza we had a great lunch at a winery and were reminded that a locally grown, whole onion, when smoked on a wood grille, is just spectacular; and, try grilling an acorn squash – soft, silky, smokey. My stomach is growling.

But here's where the businessperson in me gets all confused. If we know that different cultures and experiences lead to a new and improved and expanded view of the world, why do so many businesses not embrace diversity at all levels?

As a female business owner and board member, I regularly have a different perspective from a room full of men; conference and board rooms are still mostly white men. I'm experienced enough not to get fussy or bitter when I'm asked, again, whose assistant I am or if my husband is my business partner. My plethora of male business friends just don't have that experience, unless they are not white. If you've read my first book, you'll know that details and I don't get along, so if you don't believe the imbalance, just look up the top 50 companies in your city and browse their leadership teams and boards. Things are improving, but the imbalance is still huge and, the result is a small bubble mindset, lack of broad and deep solutions at the great majority of small and large companies.

Thanks to stupid comments, assumptions and, on occasion, inappropriate actions, I've become more aware and intentional about how I speak and act, not wanting anyone to remember an experience with me as an example of how not to be.

In early 2023, I am 57. I forget this at times, forget I'm not

30 and cool and on top of the latest technology. I listen to my young adult children and know I'm one bad comment away from being referred to as a boomer, when I use the wrong verb or mispronounce the latest-greatest tech gadget. I smile, knowing I will, at least, provide them with some funny stories to share with their friends: 'get this, my Mom said she would gladly put pictures of her feet on only fans for $50.' (If you don't know what I'm talking about, cautiously google on fans. WTF!

Acknowledgements

Thank you to my helicopter flight instructors: Jeff, Reid, Joel, and Levi. Your unyielding attention to details and obsession with flying with fluency, I believe, kept me from making a terrible mistake. You also showed me how to be patient in challenging situations and taught me to follow a very specific process, every time. Thank you to John C. Tune traffic and fuel. I was constantly amazed by your professionalism and focus on the task at hand.

To Tim Shaver who saw who I could be and, without any strings attached, challenged, and guided me to be a business owner. Without your unconditional support I would never have known a business leader version of me existed. Thank you for introducing me to her!

To my dear friends, Mara Hemminger, Carole Flodin, Melanie Bialko Leeth, Mariche Hayduk, Kimberly and Michael Bess, Joleyn Smithing, Steven Smithing, Kat Wenzler, Lori King, Kevin Clouse, Reggie Ford, Shan Foster, Cynthia Whitfield Story, Sandy Gennaro, Melissa Hudson Gant, and Dustin Dowdy. Thanks for laughing at my jokes, even when you didn't get them and for listening to my seemingly endless need to suggest you 'go with me' somewhere, experience something new with me or to vent about social justice and inequities. Thank you for encouraging me when I stirred the pot and took risks to promote a cause.

To the people I feel like I know, but don't, whose books and podcasts I've devoured and shared: Patrick Lencioni, Brené Brown, Tim Ferris, Dr. Mark Hyman, Shankar Vedantam, Cal Newport, Gino Wickman, Verne Harnish, Donald Sinclaire, Adam Grant, Cicely Tyson, Cy Wakeman, Viola Davis, Simon Sinek, Annie Duke,

Patty McCord, and The Arbinger Institute.

To my brothers, Stuart and C.R.. Thank you for always having my back and being there regardless of what whacky ideas I had. Thank you for sharing your incredible children with me and for being amazing uncles to mine.

To my board bosses, Agenia Clark (Girl Scouts of Middle Tennessee), Carlisle Carroll and Melissa Hudson Gant (Big Brothers Big Sisters of Middle Tennessee), Heather Cunningham and Sarah Lingo (Sister Cities of Nashville), Nora Kern (Walk Bike Nashville), Dominique Arrieta (Gobbell Hayes Partners), Mark Fortune (Private Directors Association), Scott and Randy Hearon and Rodes Hart (Nashville Coaching Coalition), DeLisa Guerrier (Storyville Gardens), Mark Fortune (Private Directors Association) and Tony Majors (Major League Baseball's Nashville RBI Chapter). Thank each of you for setting a high bar, trusting me, modeling how to serve others first and encouraging an abundance mindset. You also taught me that there is plenty to go around and that our job is to help people by giving of our networks, money, time, and love.

To my Vistage pals, and chair Rod Thurley who taught me that I could hold two opposing thoughts in my head with equal curiosity.

To my rocks: my husband, Michael, who listened every single time I asked him how a sentence or chapter sounded and continuously told me to keep writing. To my children, Tyson, Lucas, and Lilly. You inspire and motivate me and make me so proud.

To Radnor Lake, Percy Warner Park, The Arboretum, Fiery Gizzard, The Grand Canyon, and Grand Tetons, some of the many places where Nature soothed and nurtured me, showing me that I was both mighty and fragile as she, mother nature, is.

To my ISTS team who supported me on this journey, allowing me to transition from working in the business to on it, especially Matt Rompala and Munyette Moore who trusted me and allowed me to explore my next career without too much worry. To Jen Fisher whose genius of wonder helped me to go deeper and who stepped into project after project anytime I needed her help.

To Julie Schoerke-Gallagher whose enthusiasm, encouragement and brilliance kept me writing!

And finally, to Professor Steve Posovac, who suggested I write this. Thank you for trusting me in your classroom and with your students. Your encouragement motivated me more than I think you know.

ABOUT THE AUTHOR

Becky Scott Sharpe

Becky Sharpe's passion is to help people grow. She is a CEO and business owner, where her focus is on effective leadership and innovation through the lens of continuous growth.

When she is not working or speaking to groups of all sizes, she enjoys hiking, cycling, gardening, international travel and has recently become a certified yoga instructor. Becky is married to Michael and is the mother to three young adults to whom she regularly speaks in German. Her go-to karaoke song is Patsy Cline's Walking After Midnight.

Instagram
instagram.com/a.sharper.you

LinkedIn
linkedin.com/in/bsharpe1

PRAISE FOR AUTHOR

"Becky shares her own diverse life experiences that has shaped how she leads, parents, and gives of herself to all who come into contact with her. She challenges the best in us while nurturing the areas we've taken for granted. The balance of business and personal leaves you eager to experience the next page in her journey, and you walk away inspired, empowered, and a little better than before! And just maybe you'll find your own three words!"

- SHAN FOSTER, CEO/FOUNDER, FOSTERING HEALTHY SOLUTIONS HTTPS://FOSTERINGHEALTHYSOLUTIONS.COM/

"Unlock the power of self-reflection and unleash your full potential with this inspiring guide to journaling. Becky Sharpe's book, Three Words, is a gift that reminds us to recognize our own greatness while also highlights blind spots that may be hindering us. With its fantastic storytelling and timeless wisdom, this book has the power to transform the way you think and live."

- REGGIE D. FORD, ENTREPRENEUR, MOTIVATIONAL SPEAKER, AND BESTSELLING AUTHOR OF PERSEVERANCE THROUGH SEVERE DYSFUNCTION

"Becky's short, concise page-turner of a book provides interesting new

insights and techniques on how to be the best version of yourself, both personally and professionally. She also reminds us of life's basic principles, too often overlooked amidst our busy lives. I am fortunate to call Becky my friend and my inspiration who oozes positivity.

My "Three Words" for Becky Sharpe: Compassionate, Loving, and Focused.

I highly recommend "Three Words" to all no matter where you are on life's journey."

- SANDY GENNARO, 'THE ROCK AND ROLL THOUGHT LEADER, DRUMMER, MOTIVATIONAL SPEAKER AND AUTHOR OF BEAT THE ODDS IN BUSINESS & LIFE

www.ingramcontent.com/pod-product-compliance
Lightning Source LLC
Chambersburg PA
CBHW071355090426
42738CB00012B/3131